ESCAPING ALCATRAZ

BY CHRISTINE EVANS

The Child's World®
childsworld.com

Published by The Child's World®
1980 Lookout Drive • Mankato, MN 56003-1705
800-599-READ • www.childsworld.com

Photographs ©: Supannee Hickman/Shutterstock Images, cover, 1; Shutterstock Images, 5, 8; Golden Gate National Recreation Area/National Park Service, 6, 25; Everett Historical/Shutterstock Images, 9; Golden Gate National Recreation Area/Betty Wallar Collection/National Park Service, 10; Golden Gate National Recreation Area/Alcatraz Historic Register Nomination Photos/National Park Service, 13; Nat Farbman/The LIFE Picture Collection/Getty Images, 15; Golden Gate National Recreation Area/Kucera AZ Photo Collection/National Park Service, 16; Golden Gate National Recreation Area/Interpretation Negatives Collection/National Park Service, 18; Golden Gate National Recreation Area/McPherson/Weed Family Alcatraz Collection/National Park Service, 19; Pictorial Parade/Hulton Archive/Archive Photos/Getty Images, 22; Album/Prisma/Newscom, 26; N-CB/AP Images, 28

ISBN 9781503825253
LCCN 2017959688

Printed in the United States of America
PA02377

TABLE OF CONTENTS

FAST FACTS

- Alcatraz is a former prison on a rocky island in San Francisco Bay, California. It is surrounded by the Pacific Ocean. Alcatraz's nickname is "The Rock."
- Alcatraz Island is approximately 1,700 feet (518 m) long and 580 feet (177 m) wide. It is 1.5 miles (2.4 km) from the city of San Francisco.
- Alcatraz opened as a federal prison for men in 1934. It closed in 1963.
- The average cell in Alcatraz was 5 feet (1.5 m) wide by 9 feet (2.7 m) deep. There were four cellblocks in the prison. A Block was used for storage. B and C Blocks housed most of the inmates. D Block was for **solitary confinement**.
- In total, 1,545 inmates served time in The Rock. There were, on average, 260 inmates in the prison at any one time.
- There were 14 escape attempts by 36 inmates. Eight men died, and 23 were recaptured. Five disappeared in San Francisco Bay or were swept out into the Pacific Ocean. Those five inmates were presumed dead.

Today, Alcatraz Island is open to the public as a national park. ▶

Chapter 1

THE FIRST ESCAPE ATTEMPT

The freezing cold winds whipped Joseph Bowers's face. He was an inmate at Alcatraz and could only dream of freedom as he gazed out at the city across the bay. It was April 27, 1936, and he was working **incinerator** duty. He was sorting through piles of rotting garbage in order to burn them. At that moment, Joe couldn't bear to stay behind bars any longer. He rolled up his pants and took off his shoes. Then he climbed the chain-link fence toward the barbed wire at the top.

Joe had arrived at Alcatraz on September 4, 1934. He stepped off the boat and looked at the stark buildings, knowing it would be years before he'd make the return journey to San Francisco. Joe had been sentenced to 25 years at Alcatraz for stealing $16 from a post office. It was a time of high crime in the United States. Joe was considered a serious menace to public safety.

◄ **Inmates were guarded at all times, even during meals.**

▲ Six guard towers surrounded the prison and allowed officers to keep watch over the island.

On that blustery day in April 1936, Officer E. F. Chandler was on duty in the guard tower overlooking the yard where Joe was working. Chandler had been on his feet for hours, watching for boats straying too close to the island or an inmate wandering out of bounds. As he looked down at the yard again, he saw Joe climbing the fence. Chandler yelled at him to get down. But Joe kept climbing. Chandler prepared his rifle. He fired twice into the air as a warning.

The **warden** heard the shots. He sounded the escape siren. Joe hauled himself over the top of the fence, barbed wire cutting his hands. But he didn't stop. Freedom was yards away.

Chandler knew he couldn't let Joe escape. He took aim at Joe's legs and pulled the trigger. Joe fell to the rocks on the free side of the fence. He was the first inmate to attempt to escape Alcatraz, and it had cost him his life.

ALCATRAZ IN 1938

511
511

Chapter 2

MISSING FOR DAYS

Fog shrouded Alcatraz Island on the morning of April 13, 1943. Inmate Floyd Hamilton could barely see the waves lapping at the jagged rocks along the shore. It was perfect weather to conceal an escape.

Floyd, James Boarman, Harold Brest, and Fred Hunter had been plotting for weeks as they worked together in the machine shop. They stole fuel cans to use as floats. They also stole four army uniforms from the prison laundry. The uniforms had been sent from the nearby Angel Island army base to be cleaned by the inmates. The fuel cans were the perfect place to hide the stolen uniforms. Once they reached dry land, they would pry open the cans and dress in the uniforms to escape into the city undetected. In addition to the cans, the inmates had hidden tools to cut open the steel mesh covering the window in the machine shop.

On that foggy morning in April 1943, the four men were prepared. They went to the machine shop and started working.

◄ **Many Alcatraz inmates worked manual labor jobs in the tailor or machine shops.**

They sneaked glances out the window. Patches of blue sky were starting to appear. If they waited much longer, there wouldn't be enough fog to obscure their escape.

At last, the officer watching the men left the room to escort more inmates to work. The men quickly stripped to their underwear, kicked off their boots, and collected their cans. They hid behind the door, waiting for the officer to come back. As the officer reentered the room, the inmates jumped out, knocking him to the ground. Shortly after, the inmates heard footsteps echoing outside the machine shop door. The inmates pounced on a second officer as he entered.

The prison officers looked on, bound and gagged, as the inmates cut a hole in the mesh on the window. The inmates managed to squeeze two cans out the window, but it was taking too long. Floyd told his **accomplices** to leave behind the two remaining cans. One by one, the men slid down an iron post onto the cliffs below. They each took a deep breath and leaped into the icy water. Harold and James clutched floats. Floyd clung to a plank of wood he'd found outside. Fred treaded water to keep afloat.

Officer Frank Johnson was on duty in the guard tower. He peered through the clearing fog. He saw four inmates swimming.

The machine shop was in the Model Industries Building on Alcatraz Island. ▶

Johnson raised his gun, fired several shots at them, and sounded the escape siren. Officers scrambled to the prison boat and launched into the bay. Johnson kept firing. His bullets pelted the water around the inmates.

One of Johnson's bullets struck James's head. James sank under the dark waves of the bay. Officers on the prison boat pulled up next to Harold, who was swimming nearby, and hauled him into the vessel.

Prison officers, police, and the U.S. Coast Guard patrolled the Alcatraz shoreline for the remaining inmates. A flashlight shone on a smear of blood on a rock outside a cave. Officers found Fred, shivering and neck-deep in water, inside the cave. Fred had strained his back during the jump and didn't have the strength to swim against the strong currents. He had turned back to Alcatraz Island and crawled into the cave.

The officers kept searching for Floyd, but the fourth escapee had vanished. Warden James A. Johnston concluded Floyd must have also been shot and drowned in the bay. But the warden was wrong. Floyd shivered behind a boulder in the same cave where Fred had been found. He eventually realized he wouldn't be able make it across the bay.

▲ Officers used boats to search for escaped inmates in San Francisco Bay.

After three days in the cave, Floyd gave up. He hauled himself back up the cliff he'd leaped from, back up the iron post, and through the window into the machine shop. He hid in a storeroom. Prison officers found him cowering in tattered clothes, covered in cuts, and weak from extreme cold and hunger.

Despite their careful planning, Floyd, James, Harold, and Fred's escape attempt ended with three men in solitary confinement and one man dead.

Chapter 3

THE BATTLE OF ALCATRAZ

On May 2, 1946, Alcatraz inmate Bernard Coy pushed a broom along the concrete cell house floor near the C-Block cells. He looked up at the gun gallery, a caged area above the cells where an armed officer kept watch over the inmates. Officer Bert Burch had finally left to patrol D Block. The clock in the hallway read 1:38 p.m. It was time to execute the escape plan.

Inmate Marvin Hubbard had finished cleaning the kitchen. He slid a kitchen knife up his sleeve. The sharp, cold blade pressed against his skin as he headed back to the main cell house. Officer William Miller was on duty at the cell house door. He opened the door and patted Marvin down, searching for stolen items. Bernard swept closer to the officer and seized his chance. He punched Miller in the back of the head. Marvin hit the officer's face. Miller crumpled to the ground.

◀ Each cellblock in Alcatraz contained two rows and three levels of cells.

▲ Inmate Bernard Coy was sentenced to 25 years at Alcatraz for bank robbery.

Marvin and Bernard tied up Miller and dragged him into a cell in C Block. Bernard took Miller's keys and rushed to the control panel to unlock the C-Block cells. Two accomplices, Joseph Cretzer and Clarence Carnes, walked out of their cells.

▲ **The warden lived near the lighthouse on Alcatraz Island.**

The men moved fast. One inmate had made a tool to spread apart the bars of the gun gallery. This bar spreader was made of pipes from a toilet, a nut, and a wrench. Bernard grabbed the bar spreader from the C-Block utility corridor, where he'd stashed it. Next, Joseph smeared slimy axle grease on Bernard's body. Bernard started to climb the gun gallery with the cold metal bar spreader clenched in his teeth. When he reached the top, he wedged the spreader between the bars. He turned the wrench.

The bars spread apart. Bernard sucked in his stomach and squeezed his greasy body through the 10-inch (25-cm) gap.

Bernard waited behind the door of the gun gallery. A few minutes later, Burch returned. He opened the door to the gallery. Bernard knocked the officer out with a club he'd found in the gun gallery. Then Bernard tossed clubs and guns to the inmates waiting below.

Within the next 20 minutes, the inmates captured seven more officers and forced them into one C-Block cell. Meanwhile, Bernard unlocked the D-Block cells. Inmates Samuel Shockley and Miran Thompson joined the hopeful escapees.

By 2:00 p.m., the officer in charge of the **armory** had a feeling something was wrong. Officer Cliff Fish picked up his phone and called the C-Block officer. There was no answer. He called the D-Block officer. No answer. So at 2:07 p.m., Fish turned on the escape siren. The siren's wail echoed across the island. The escapees knew then that they were trapped.

Meanwhile, Warden Johnston worked on a plan to rescue the hostages. He summoned the U.S. Coast Guard, Marines, and officers from nearby prisons to help. They raced across the bay in boats and surrounded The Rock.

An assault team armed with guns and flashlights entered the prison and located the hostages. Bernard fired at the officers.

Bullets rained on them, but they returned fire. The officers managed to rescue all nine hostages, carrying the injured out of the dark building to safety.

Marines drilled holes in the roof and tossed in **tear gas** grenades. The grenades filled the cellblock with thick smoke. But Bernard and his group still refused to surrender.

Finally, after nearly 48 hours had passed, the gunshots from the inmates stopped. Officers entered the battleground to find the bodies of Joseph, Bernard, and Marvin in a corridor. The men had died from bullet and **shrapnel** wounds. The Battle of Alcatraz was over. The officers had won.

AFTERMATH

In the aftermath of the Battle of Alcatraz, only three of Bernard's accomplices survived. Miran and Samuel were later sentenced to death because they had killed two prison officers during the riot. Clarence was sentenced to an additional 99 years in prison. The bullet holes on the prison walls reminded all inmates of the consequences of attempted escape from The Rock. Today, visitors to Alcatraz Island can still see bullet holes in the area where the battle occurred.

Chapter 4

THE MYSTERY OF ALCATRAZ

At 9:30 p.m. on June 11, 1962, Alcatraz prison officers finished the bedtime inmate count in B Block. They turned off the lights. Four inmates hid a secret as they huddled under their blankets in their cold cells. Tonight, they would escape.

Frank Morris, Allen West, and brothers John and Clarence Anglin had long been plotting their escape. Their cells were next to each other in a row on B Block. Frank realized that breaking through the air vents on the back wall of their cells and climbing into the utility corridor beyond was their best chance for escape. So each night, they waited until after the head count at 5:30 p.m. That was when inmates were allowed free time to play musical instruments. The sounds of music drowned out the sounds of the men chipping away at the concrete around the air vents in their cells. The men used metal spoons stolen from the dining hall.

◀ **Inmate Frank Morris was the mastermind behind the June 11, 1962, escape attempt from Alcatraz.**

They also used drill bits stolen from the prison workshop. They got rid of the concrete dust by flushing it down the toilets in their cells or hiding it in their coat pockets and dropping it outside at exercise time. They used soap mixed with toilet paper to plug the holes in the wall. They even painted pieces of cardboard to look like the air vents to disguise their work.

The men constructed fake heads to use as decoys, or models meant to fool the guards. They mixed soap with toilet paper and plaster from the wall chippings to make the heads. Inmates were allowed to have art supplies, so the men ordered paint and brushes. They painted the heads to resemble each inmate. They even added real hair collected from the prison barber shop.

Once the holes in the back of their cells were big enough, they squeezed through and climbed the water pipes into an overhead space. This area became their workshop. They left the decoy heads in their beds to fool the prison officers. In their workshop, they made a raft and life vests from 50 stolen raincoats. They also made wooden paddles from plywood. The paddles would help them steer the raft across the bay.

After months of work, the four men were ready. They placed their decoy heads on their beds. They fluffed up their pillows and tucked them under the covers to look like their bodies. Frank and the Anglin brothers climbed up the pipes to their workshop.

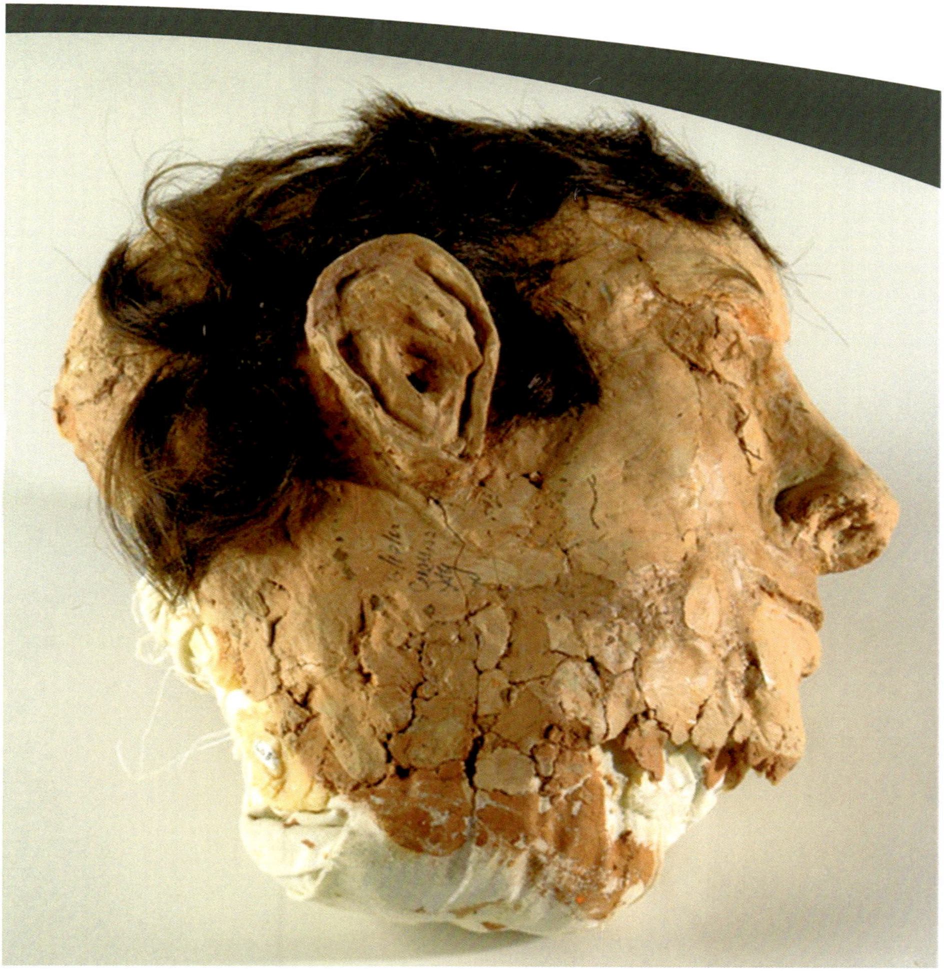

▲ Frank Morris and his accomplices each made a decoy head to fool the guards.

They hauled their raft, vests, and paddles through a ventilator shaft and climbed onto the prison's roof. They gazed at the lights of San Francisco shining across the bay. Freedom was almost within their grasp.

Back in his cell, Allen frantically chipped away at the concrete around his vent. But the vent was stuck. The others couldn't wait. They left behind a vest for Allen. Then they climbed down a chimney, over a fence, and down to the island's shore. They launched their raft into the treacherous waters of the bay.

THE ESCAPEES

Frank Morris began his criminal career as a teenager, when he was convicted for armed robberies and drug possession. Before arriving at Alcatraz, Frank had escaped from a prison in Louisiana. He was recaptured and brought to Alcatraz in 1960. John and Clarence Anglin had been bank robbers. Both made failed escape attempts from a prison in Atlanta, Georgia, and were afterward sent to Alcatraz. Allen West had been convicted for stealing cars, and he was transferred to Alcatraz in 1957 after a failed escape attempt from a prison in Florida.

◄ Frank Morris and his accomplices escaped through the vents in the back of their cells.

▲ **The U.S. Coast Guard used boats and a helicopter to search for Frank Morris and his accomplices.**

In the morning, an alarm sounded to wake the inmates. But Frank wasn't stirring. Officer Lawrence Bartlett went into Frank's cell. He nudged what he thought was Frank's sleeping body. Frank's decoy head rolled to the ground, its nose breaking on the concrete floor. Once Bartlett recovered from the shock, he raised the alarm.

The escape siren wailed. The prison went into **lockdown**. Dogs tracked the men's scent to the water's edge. Then the U.S. Coast Guard searched the bay for any sign of the escapees.

The Federal Bureau of Investigation (FBI) hunted for clues along the shorelines of Alcatraz, San Francisco, and nearby Angel Island. They discovered a sealed packet of letters, some pieces of wood, and a homemade life vest. But the men had vanished.

Many theories have suggested Frank Morris and his accomplices survived their escape attempt. There have been many alleged sightings. But the FBI says there is no evidence the men made it to dry land. The FBI closed its investigation in 1979 and turned the case over to the U.S. Marshals Service. The U.S. Marshals continue to look for answers about what happened to the escapees.

THINK ABOUT IT

- Inmates who didn't follow rules or tried to escape were often put in solitary confinement. Do you think such punishment was justified? Why or why not?
- Some men died or were injured while trying to escape from Alcatraz. Why do you think inmates kept trying to escape in spite of these dangers?
- What do you think Alcatraz would be like today if it were still a prison?

GLOSSARY

accomplices (uh-KOM-pliss-ez): Accomplices are people who help someone else commit a crime. Some Alcatraz inmates, such as Bernard Coy, had accomplices to help them escape.

armory (AR-mur-ee): An armory is a place where weapons are stored. In Alcatraz, an officer guarded the armory, which stored the officers' weapons.

incinerator (in-SIN-uh-ray-tur): An incinerator is a furnace used to burn garbage. Incinerator duty was one of the many jobs inmates had at Alcatraz.

lockdown (LOK-down): Lockdown is the confining of inmates to their cells when there is a disturbance or an escape is in progress. When the prison officers found out Frank Morris and his accomplices had escaped, they put the prison into lockdown.

shrapnel (SHRAP-nuhl): Shrapnel are fragments of metal created after an explosion. Exploding grenades released shrapnel during the battle of Alcatraz.

solitary confinement (SOL-uh-tair-ee kuhn-FINE-muhnt): Solitary confinement is the complete isolation of an inmate in a cell as punishment. When Alcatraz inmates broke a rule or tried to escape, they were often put in solitary confinement.

tear gas (TEER GASS): Tear gas is a type of gas that causes severe eye and skin irritation. Officers attacked Bernard Coy and his accomplices with tear gas grenades during the battle of Alcatraz.

warden (WOR-duhn): A warden is a person in charge of an entire prison. Warden James A. Johnston was the first warden of Alcatraz.

TO LEARN MORE

Books

Bakker, T. C. *Alcatraz: Believe It or Not.* San Francisco, CA: Golden Gate National Parks Conservancy, 2016.

Gordon, Nick. *Alcatraz.* Minneapolis, MN: Bellwether, 2014.

Nagelhout, Ryan. *Haunted! Alcatraz.* New York, NY: Gareth Stevens, 2014.

Web Sites

Visit our Web site for links about escapes from Alcatraz:
childsworld.com/links

Note to Parents, Teachers, and Librarians: We routinely verify our Web links to make sure they are safe and active sites. So encourage your readers to check them out!

SELECTED BIBLIOGRAPHY

Babyak, Jolene. *Breaking the Rock: The Great Escape from Alcatraz.* Berkeley, CA: Ariel Vamp Press, 2001. Print.

Bruce, J. Campbell. *Escape from Alcatraz.* Berkeley, CA: Ten Speed Press, 2005. Print.

Esslinger, Michael. *Alcatraz: A History of the Penitentiary Years.* San Francisco, CA: Ocean View, 2016. Print.

Johnston, James A. *Alcatraz Island Prison and the Men Who Live There.* New York, NY: Charles Scribner's Sons, 1949. Print.

INDEX

ABOUT THE AUTHOR

Christine Evans is a freelance writer based in San Jose, California. She writes children's books and stories for magazines, including *Highlights*. She lives with her husband, two daughters, and a tiny dog. Christine loves writing about historical adventures like the daring escapes in this book.